Without My Son
A Memoir of Parental Alienation and Coercive Control

MARCIA LEAVY

DEDICATION

These words are written to bring awareness to the experience of intimate partner violence and domestic abuse victims who have been intentionally betrayed by law enforcement and officers of the court.

Without My Son: A Memoir of Parental Alienation and Coercive Control is dedicated to those victims of Domestic Abuse and Judicial Misconduct who had their voices silenced with no recourse of action to compensate for the injustices that they have suffered. This book is written for *The Invalidated*.

CONTENTS

Table of Contents

ACKNOWLEDGMENTS

My respect and appreciation for my son, Suni Smith
for encouraging me to fight are beyond measure. I am
grateful for him because when I was weak
emotionally and financially, he supported me and
wouldn't allow me to give up. When I was low on
funds he helped me to soothe his sister when we had
to go without.

Thank you to my daughter, Marseille Smith who
reminded me to focus on the good things in my life.

To my mother who transitioned in 2020, you have
shown me the meaning of unconditional love and
what it truly means to be a dedicated mother.

1 NUANCES

I paid for my freedom with my son when I decided to flee the overbearing relationship that I was involved in with my former husband. I survived abuse that was sexual, psychological, and financial. From the beginning of our relationship, there were red flags. He had confidence issues and was insecure. Although very intelligent and considered attractive, he struggled with his self-esteem. He felt entitled to control me but was not equipped to maintain control over himself. He lacked discipline and the ability to regulate his own emotions.

After divorcing him, I decided to remain cordial and friendly with him, which was a big mistake. He stalked me, violated my privacy, and used technology to keep tabs on me. I failed to establish healthy boundaries with him. Following our divorce he would often stop by my home unannounced and uninvited. He would call me on the phone and would hold me hostage for hours. I felt nauseous when I thought of him and I knew that this post-marital connection was not healthy for me or my children. I wanted to remove his demanding presence in my life, so I decided it would be best to create as much distance between us as possible.

His unwanted sexual advances and ongoing obsession with me made me feel unsafe. His criticisms of the children and the constant emotional manipulations that he subjected them to gave me no choice but to attempt to secure our safety and well-being absent of his presence.

I made plans to move out of state and far away from him and his toxic ways. What is the proper procedure for prey to realistically escape the crosshairs of their hunter who is locked in on them and determined to triumph over them to cause malice and to strategize on their demise?

I can not fully explain why I never filed police reports on the multiple times that he raped me. I can not fully explain why I did not hate him and did not want to see him get what he deserved. Like many victims of abuse, I struggled with self-worth. My lack of self-value to hold him accountable for all he had done was part of the issue. The other part was the errors in judgment that I had made. Ignoring the red flags, and being submissive to a partner who didn't earn my devotion or respect are a few of my missteps.

I can acknowledge my error in my choice of partner, and to correct my poor decision, I believed that the right thing to do was to put my children's well-being above my own by suffering in silence...another mistake. My perception that I couldn't have one without the other was where I went wrong. Just because I made a mistake does not mean I deserved perpetual punishment or that my children could only experience joy if I remained in union with their father. My children's success was not tied to me suffering alongside their father as his narcissistic supply.

So much time went by that I had convinced myself that it didn't matter what he had done to me. In retrospect, I know now that my decision not to pursue charges against him for the crimes that he had committed against me was equivalent to conceding that I did not matter.

It took time for me to heal and to learn that how I chose to diminish the severity of my situation was not healthy. It was a trauma response that I relied on to cope with surviving my abusive situation. I feared my ability to provide for my children. I beat myself up about contributing to the negative societal stereotypes. I didn't want to be a single mom. I didn't want to live in poverty. I wanted to do my best and be my best for my children. I knew that ending the abuse would expose the fact that our family was not as happy, healthy, or strong as we had led on.

2 CHESS

My decision to move out of state and not include my former husband in my plans triggered him even more. The deceit was imperative for my survival. I couldn't afford to sustain an attack that I could quite possibly not have recovered from.

He had a history of vindictiveness and indifference evidenced by him vandalizing random people's vehicles who have raged with him in traffic. Following them to their destination and then taking his frustration and anger out on their automobiles. He has a history of suicidal threats and owned firearms to carry out his moments of weakness to self-harm. When I decided to divorce him, he threatened to end his own life. If he was at risk of taking his own life, myself and my children were also at risk of having our lives taken as well.

After spying on me through surveillance and stalking, he illegally entered my home, bragged about it, and then campaigned to discredit me and assassinate my character to anyone who would listen, including my children. He eventually pled guilty to aggravated trespass with the intent to cause me bodily harm, the magistrate in our case did not take his transgression against me and others seriously and disregarded my accusation without further investigation.

Domestic violence victims who have found the courage to leave abusive relationships rely on authority figures to step in and prevent harmful situations from escalating. The inability of the magistrate to detect danger or recognize the signs of abuse and take appropriate action could be categorized as incompetence or malpractice in my estimation.

The magistrate's failure to make an effort to ensure the safety of the mother of the children involved in a case under her supervision taught me that I have to be a champion for myself regardless of the air of self-righteousness that some people in positions of power project. I have learned that there may be times when these exalted "Lords of Justice" will be wrong and that sometimes they will never take accountability for their actions. Although these individuals have been granted the extreme control and power to impact the lives of many, it doesn't mean that the outcome of my life or who I am must be defined by the mistakes they've made.

My former husband attempted to insert himself into my new life and decided to sabotage my plans to relocate. He shared that eventually, he would join us in Georgia, agreeing to split holidays and have summer visitations with the children until he made the move. I was completely fine with the visitation agreement but was hoping that he would get distracted by another woman and forget all about me and his intentions to follow me down south.

As we stood face-to-face, negotiating our new visitation agreement, I remained friendly and diplomatic so he wouldn't plummet into an emotional tirade. I didn't think forcing him to accept that his offer of a romantic relationship was absurd would be productive. I didn't want to make him upset or give him a reason to become adversarial. It was a challenge to tap dance and tip-toe around the fragile emotions of someone desperate for acceptance and validation.

In the past, his manipulations worked on me. But I was beyond done with him and his plan to entice me by sweetening the pot with the offer to buy me a new home. It didn't work. This most likely marks when he may have become suspicious of me and my true intentions to ditch him. I was on public assistance and still trying to become financially stable. He knew that I had spent every penny I had on my upcoming move to Georgia, and he knew that my deepest desire was to have the stability of owning my own home.

3 WISH

My rejection of his offer undoubtedly prompted my former husband to allow his curiosity to encourage him to violate my privacy; he had convinced himself that I was leaving town to run away with another man. Yes, I began to avoid him and stopped allowing him to cross the boundaries that I had established. But it wasn't because of another man, it was because I was on my healing journey. I was learning how to love and value myself. He was accustomed to me neglecting myself for him, so he assumed that another relationship was why I was abandoning him. He had lost my affection, respect, and desire to stay connected to him before our divorce in 2011.

My former husband and I had maintained a platonic relationship for several years following the birth of our daughter in 2013. He continued to try to win me back, but I made it clear to him that we would never be together again, he was convinced that he could change my mind. Based on his delusions that he concluded by stalking me and spying on me he went to court to prevent me from moving away. He believed that he could use my children as a tool to force me to stay. By this time the tides had turned and I got my wish, only I thought that it would be another woman who would make him lose interest in me.

It seems that as a result of his spying on me, he became appalled at whom he assumed that he was replaced by and the delusions transformed his obsession to own me into his obsession to despise me. Since he couldn't manipulate me into coming back to him, he initiated his new plan which was to in his own words "cripple me financially so that I wouldn't have any other choice but to come crawling back to him."

He made true to his promise. My finances were destroyed. He stopped paying child support for my children and used the withholding of income as a weapon in an attempt to control me once again. I underestimated the ego death he may have been experiencing, let alone the desperation that he demonstrated when he activated his most lethal aggression of violence against me when he used our children to exact his revenge and reciprocate the pain that I unintentionally inflicted on him.

With all that transpired, I granted him an unscheduled visitation with our 2 youngest children to go trick-or-treating on Halloween of 2018. I arrived at my former husband's residence to collect the children. He only returned my daughter. He sent his parents to tell me he was not returning my son. I outstayed my lease and waited in Ohio for over a week to retrieve my son without success. I contacted the local police department and initially did receive assistance. They contacted my ex and connected with his attorney. I would not become aware of the reputation of his attorney, which is nothing less than disgraceful and deplorable until I faced her in person during pre-trial discussions. She was the perfect vindictive narc attorney for the most indignant narc client.

It is sad and disheartening to be in the presence of an individual who is morally challenged and uses their knowledge of the legal system to exploit legal loopholes and ruin lives. This attorney uses her expertise and talent as an opportunity to perpetuate dishonesty and to be conniving. I've watched the movies and heard the horror stories and relentless jokes about the character flaws of lawyers.

I never considered that one day I would interact with someone who masquerades as human but is the opposite. This individual communicated to law enforcement that I had no active court order regarding the possession of our children, which was an unethical and intentional falsehood of the truth.

4 DISENFRANCHISED

Here, you have an officer of the court who blatantly lied to law enforcement which resulted in them declining to pursue assisting me with re-gaining possession of my child. These law enforcement officers took the word of a court official who by default has a self-serving interest to acquire benefits for her client.

As one would expect, this turn of events put me at a huge disadvantage. The law applied by these officers was biased and unethical. I was denied service and protection because I didn't belong to the club and failed to pay the toll to ensure lies told by opposing counsel would not go unchecked. My claims were assessed to be less valuable in comparison to their justice system colleague's. My inability to retain an attorney signaled to them that I was among the voiceless and the powerless.

Their choice to turn their back on me would go without notice. No one would ever know what they've done. Who would be the wiser? It is with the veil of not facing the ostracism of public opinion or suffering the consequences of their disloyalty to their oath that the re-traumatization of domestic abuse is likely to persist.

When I went before the magistrate, instead of compelling my former husband to comply with our parenting plan agreement she, like the police officers, suggested that I retain an attorney. I had already confided to her that I could not afford an attorney. She insulted me by regurgitating the standard script for those who obviously cannot afford an attorney because otherwise they would already be represented by an attorney. I was a domestic caregiver who wanted to part ways with her abusive partner so much that during the divorce proceedings, I elected to waive my right to spousal support. I did not want to give him a reason to prolong the process, so I walked away with nothing. I recognize several mistakes that I have made in my choice of partnership. However, the magistrate's decision to ignore the visitation schedule that was already in place is why the presence of trauma-informed support advocates is a necessity in high-conflict child custody cases.

Another mistake was believing that the court system would protect me and honor its written words to me and my family. The lesson learned in this situation is that financially vulnerable litigants can easily become re-victimized by uninformed judges and magistrates who lack trauma-informed judicial practice. My former husband failed to petition the court to change the terms of our agreement before withholding my son from me and the magistrate allowed it. This failure to follow procedure forced me into a position where my status informally shifted from primary caregiver to non-custodial parent.

My problem was that I had a magistrate who knew

my weakness. She knew I needed more financial resources and proper knowledge of court procedures and rules. Although I filed a motion to show cause for my former husband failing to adhere to the established visitation schedule, this magistrate ignored the conditions outlined in my family's agreement and refused to enforce the order. She didn't respect the ruling of the previous magistrate and she simply pretended that the parenting agreement didn't exist. I assert that she did this because she was not equipped to fulfill the tasks associated with conducting a proper trial that would meet the standards outlined for her professional position.

The terms of our agreement were clear and this magistrate did not care. Therefore, my son was unlawfully ripped away from me because the magistrate used her knowledge of the system to violate my rights. I could not afford to pay someone to assist me with my legal situation and the magistrate did not respect me enough to allow me to advocate for myself and I was made to feel powerless. I had to accept assistance from wherever I could get it.

I didn't know what to do and played the only position available to me, which was to be a spectator at my own sporting event. Even after acquiring a legal aid attorney I felt oppressed and re-victimized by the system. My counsel was a puppet for the magistrate and she was a disloyal, treacherous infiltrator.

The magistrate assigned to our case knew exactly what she was doing when she aided my former husband in alienating my son from me. She participated in the family court process daily, therefore she knew what would be the outcome of her decision not to enforce the court-ordered parenting agreement. She decided to use her knowledge and power to deprive me of my son.

5 CONSPIRACY

Beaten down, alone, financially fragile, and emotionally weak...he had done it. He had essentially destroyed me as he said that he would. I was more devastated by the judicial system's role than his actions because I expected this behavior from him. I did not anticipate this type of treatment from the court system. I felt that I had escaped him. I was proud of myself for breaking free. But I never thought his secret weapon against me would be that of the Family Court Judiciary.

One might think that a system based on law, order, specialized education, and a legitimized foundation would result in a certain level of competency and consistency. In my experience, I felt that the system did not care about me or my children. I learned that these "invested parties", judges, attorneys, and law enforcement only care about themselves and their bottom line. The culture of the judicial system can be duplicitous and a fabrication of reality with the use of words like "fair, just, and equality" to create blind faith among the public as a system that has failed to live up to its promises. What I was not aware of is that by my ex unlawfully withholding my son, he was accomplishing multiple key advantages for himself that would be beneficial to his goal to hack the family court system.

The first advantage is that the magistrate and his attorney knew through their experience with family court that if my son remained with my ex over an extended period whether by legal means or not, the custody order that was already in place could become obsolete and essentially be reduced to worthlessness because by my son being permitted to be re-homed with his father and not residing with myself and his siblings that the court would conclude that the child is established at school, has friends and could determine that it is not in the best interest in the child to disrupt their life.

The big revelation I have uncovered is that just like in politics there are loopholes within the family court paradigm. Similar to gerrymandering, withholding a child and alienating them from the other parent creates an inauthentic dynamic that supports a biased outcome. Instead of going through the proper channels of filing to change parental rights, my ex was supported by the magistrate to get around this process by using her position to aid him in withholding my son from me.

I have been my children's primary caregiver since their births. My ex wanted to avoid financially contributing to my ability to move on with my life and the magistrate allowed him to use coercive controlling tactics and the power of the courts to cause additional trauma, pain, and suffering in my life. It is my opinion that my former husband and his attorney could only be successful in this unlawful alienation of my son with the assistance of the magistrate who was aware of these dynamics when she failed to enforce the pre-established order.

Another advantage was him finding a way to cut off my financial support which was crucial to his plan. In addition to not receiving the court-ordered child support awarded to me, I was forced to participate in 2 child custody cases within 2 separate court systems simultaneously. During this time I lost my job due to the traveling demands and strain associated with the frequency of attending court. I suffered financial ruin because I had to resort to using credit cards awaiting child support that never came.

6 DEGRADATION

This new reality of relocating to a new city, having unexpected travel, court fees, and a lack of stable income had taken a toll on my finances. It negatively impacted my credit score and began a downward spiral requiring time, attention, and resources to overcome. Not to mention the suffering and stress of keeping my head above water. If only I had someone in my corner who understood the nuances of trauma. If only legislation could assist court officials with detecting and addressing matters of coercive control, perhaps things would have been different for me.

My financial circumstances hurt me while seeking employment because of my inability to pay my debts. It called into question my creditworthiness without consideration of the systemic circumstances meddling in the background. The legal demands applied by the court, instigated by the motives of my former abusive partner, were never taken into consideration. The financial attack that I suffered created more of a challenge for me to provide for my household and create stability in the best interest of my children. Add on the grief of being alienated away from my child, in addition to the negligence of the court and the fact that my claims of abuse were completely ignored. My protest of court-related expenses I could not afford fell on deaf ears.

The magistrate was determined to execute a same-sex placement for my children. She wanted an easy solution prescribing that my son be placed with his father and my daughter placed with me. I believe her logic in this instance to be a sexist solution and it undermined the prestige of her honor as a trusted court magistrate. Her focus was absent in facilitating harmony within our family unit.

Participating in the judicial system has been the most terrifying experience of my life. My son was unlawfully taken from me by a court system that claims to be just and fair with no official reasons given for disregarding the court order which designated me as the primary caretaker.

It appears that this judiciary did not believe that I was due an explanation and that they were not obligated to offer any support as to why I had to suffer and be without my son. I don't anticipate that I will ever be granted closure to this end. Since 2018, when all of this first transpired, the family court system has failed me and deemed me undeserving to participate in my son's life.

My former husband believes that he has punished me for walking away from him and rejecting him in love, but what he has done is cause additional harm to our children. He thought that by keeping my son from me I would give in to his demands and I would sacrifice myself for my son. He didn't know that I was done betraying myself. I was no longer indulging in selflessness I had embraced selfishness for the first time in my life. What he fails to see is how our children are directly impacted by his vendetta to create chaos in my life, they are the ones who have suffered the most.

Additionally, the courts should recognize their part in facilitating the conditions that heighten abusive litigation. I have surrendered to my error in assuming my children belong to me. The magistrate and the family court system have made it very clear that I am not guaranteed parental rights as it relates to my children who I gave birth to, sacrificed for, and nurtured without regret.

Learn from my experience and you decide who should control the welfare of our children. Are the rules, laws, and procedures of our family court system appropriate, effective, and balanced? Should an external watchdog entity be in place to prevent unchecked judicial misconduct and the error of law?

Avoid making the same mistakes that I made. Use my situation as a cautionary tale. When you decide to leave your abusive partner, approach the matter with the highest level of vigilance, or else you may find yourself trapped in a pitfall more terrifying than you could have ever imagined.

7 DELIVERANCE

Some people do not understand how they contribute to victims of abuse remaining in domestic violence relationships until they are shown what they could not previously see. I hope the Court Judiciary Community will receive the sentiment of my real-life story and make the appropriate changes within their respective profession. Those who find themselves in positions of power allow "insignificant people" to become shattered by significant problems.

When I needed help and didn't know how I would make it through this devastating time, strangers came to my aid. They were sent by God I suppose. The most high showed up for me because I lacked the foresight to plan for such a disaster. I had no choice but to rely on my belief that God would protect, guide, and lead me toward brighter days.

With the support of my children, they encouraged me to maintain a positive outlook and have inspired me to be grateful that we had made it through these challenging times together. I knew that my dire circumstances would eventually change and that this period of suffering was temporary. I satisfied my self-care needs by seeking mental health assistance to address the grief and the feelings of betrayal. I remained disciplined by finding a way to turn around my financial situation.

I am determined not to allow my conflict with my ex to end me. I have looked within and surrendered to the wisdom I acquired through the lessons that I have learned. All of the positive gains that I have achieved will never erase the fact that my relationship with my son has been tarnished. It is a loss that I couldn't imagine that I will ever fully recover from, but I will continue to reflect upon it.

Some people may accuse me of not moving on, or getting over the fact that my son was stolen from me. They will claim that I cannot get over the past. I will never get over the pain that I have been caused, but I have accepted the loss of my son so that I may heal from the devastation. I had no choice but to let it go emotionally, otherwise, I would not have had the ability to be present for my other children. I desire to speak about my trauma in its entirety and alert the public of the flaws within the family court system that I experienced so that I can help others to avoid a similar outcome.

Although I recognize my issues with setting healthy boundaries in my past relationship which landed me in the position of being re-victimized by the family court system, I was incidentally made aware that there is much work to be done to correct systematic oppression as it relates to trauma-informed judicial practice.

In my case, my ex campaigned to convince everyone that he was awarded custody of my son and that I was found unfit in some way as a mother. But the truth is that because I lacked the financial resources to fight for my child in a system that values financial assets over "justice and fairness", I was denied access to him without remorse or empathy from our family court authority. My former husband was not awarded custody of our son, he simply was not compelled to follow our pre-existing court order.

There is a court-ordered visitation schedule for my daughter to visit with her father, but I received no court order for visitation with my son. The court system has proven to be unreliable, inconsistent, and unempathetic. They hung me out to dry and it is through these ominous circumstances that I was forced to experience the devastation of being brutally separated from my son. Likened to black enslaved women whose children were stolen from them and sold into chattel slavery with their maternal bonds severed, I too feel the pain of suffering through forced parental separation.

I am left to accept that as it stands today, the court officials involved in my child custody case did not value me as a citizen worthy of their best efforts and did not conclude that I deserved to claim my parental rights as a dedicated and attentive mother. I have overcome my tragic experience with the judicial system and I move forward on my journey to use my experience to inform and enlighten society. It is not my heart's desire to adopt victimhood or to make false claims of judicial misconduct. My testimony is affirmed and is supported by the fact that after all these years of protesting and pleading for a remedy, I remain to be without my son.

ABOUT THE AUTHOR

Motivated by betrayal, injustice, and pain, Marcia Leavy has embarked on a mission to transform her personal experiences into a force for systemic change. With a long history of community outreach, volunteer work, and social activism, she is committed to creating meaningful change. Marcia has contributed to the missions of prominent organizations such as The Legal Aid Society of Cleveland and the Neighborhood Leadership Institute. As an author of 4 children's books and the forthcoming work, *Intimate Partner Violence for Judges, Magistrates, and Officers of the Court: An Examination of Domestic Relations and Judicial Misconduct*, Marcia uses her experience to inform and empower. Her work reflects a deep commitment to raising awareness about abusive litigation, parental alienation, and judicial misconduct. Currently, she continues to invest in her community as the founder of TISA (Trauma Informed Support Advocates), a nonprofit organization advocating for trauma-informed judicial practice and the implementation of coercive control legislation to protect victims of domestic violence.

www.ingramcontent.com/pod-product-compliance
Lightning Source LLC
Chambersburg PA
CBHW051818050726
47598CB00006B/2605